LEARN TO

Bead Earrings

Kaia's Dream, page 18

www.companyscoming.com
visit our website

Waterfall Clusters, page 82

Learn to Bead Earrings

First Printing April 2010

Library and Archives Canada Cataloguing in Publication
Learn to bead earrings.
(Workshop series)
Includes index.
ISBN 978-1-897477-36-6
1. Earrings. 2. Beadwork. I. Title: Bead earrings.
II. Series: Workshop series (Edmonton, Alta.)
TT860.L32 2010   745.594'2   C2009-904589-3

Published by
Company's Coming Publishing Limited
2311-96 Street
Edmonton, Alberta, Canada T6N 1G3
Tel: 780-450-6223   Fax: 780-450-1857
www.companyscoming.com

Company's Coming is a registered trademark owned by Company's Coming Publishing Limited

Printed in China

The Company's Coming Story

Jean Paré grew up with an understanding that family, friends and home cooking are the key ingredients for a good life. A mother of four, Jean worked as a professional caterer for 18 years, operating out of her home kitchen. During that time, she came to appreciate quick and easy recipes that call for everyday ingredients. In answer to mounting requests for her recipes, Company's Coming cookbooks were born, and Jean moved on to a new chapter in her career.

In the beginning, Jean worked from a spare bedroom in her home, located in the

Company's Coming founder Jean Paré

small prairie town of Vermilion, Alberta, Canada. The first Company's Coming cookbook, *150 Delicious Squares*, was an immediate bestseller. Today, with well over 150 titles in print, Company's Coming has earned the distinction of publishing Canada's most popular cookbooks. The company continues to gain new supporters by adhering to Jean's "Golden Rule of Cooking"—Never share a recipe you wouldn't use yourself. It's an approach that has worked—millions of times over!

Company's Coming cookbooks are distributed throughout Canada, the United States, Australia and other international English-language markets. French and Spanish language editions have also been published. Sales to date have surpassed 25 million copies with no end in sight. Familiar and trusted in home kitchens around the world, Company's Coming cookbooks are highly regarded both as kitchen workbooks and as family heirlooms.

Just as Company's Coming continues to promote the tradition of home cooking, the same is now true with crafting. Like good cooking, great craft results depend upon easy-to-follow instructions, readily available materials and enticing photographs of the finished products. Also like cooking, crafting is meant to be enjoyed in the home or cottage. Company's Coming Crafts, then, is a natural extension from the kitchen into the family room or den.

Because Company's Coming operates a test kitchen and not a craft shop, we've partnered with a major North American craft content publisher to assemble a variety of craft compilations exclusively for us. Our editors have been involved every step of the way. You can see the excellent results for yourself in the book you're holding.

Company's Coming Crafts are for everyone—whether you're a beginner or a seasoned pro. What better gift could you offer than something you've made yourself? In these hectic days, people still enjoy crafting parties; they bring family and friends together in the same way a good meal does. Company's Coming is proud to support crafters with this new creative book series.

We hope you enjoy these easy-to-follow, informative and colourful books, and that they inspire your creativity. So, don't delay—get crafty!

TABLE OF CONTENTS

Sassy Sequin Hoops, page 48

Feelin' the Blues, page 52

In the Loop, page 34

Red Doughnuts, page 28

Luxe Lotus, page 36

TABLE OF CONTENTS

Emperor's Garden, page 90

Purple Passion Drops, page 70

Modern Holly, page 116

Dancing Stars, page 112

Make it yourself!

COMPANY'S COMING
CRAFT WORKSHOP BOOKS

CRAFT WORKSHOP SERIES

Get a craft class in a book! General instructions teach basic skills or how to apply them in a new way. Easy-to-follow steps, diagrams and photos make projects simple.

Whether paper crafting, knitting, crocheting, beading, sewing or quilting—find beautiful, fun designs you can make yourself.

For a complete listing of Company's Coming cookbooks and craft books, check out
www.companyscoming.com

FOREWORD

Beaded earrings are not only a quick way to give familiar outfits a whole new twist—they also make perfect gifts for the fashion-forward ladies in your life! As you flip through these pages you'll be sure to find the perfect design to complete any look. Like many beaders, you may already have a stash of beads and jewellery components, just waiting to create dazzling earrings you'll be proud to give or to wear.

We've included 54 stylish designs, using three skill levels ranging from beginner to intermediate. Earrings are a great way to learn the basics of jewellery making; intermediate-level projects are included for more experienced beaders, but we make it simple for you to build your skills until you can create any pair in the book.

You'll find earring designs to suit any occasion or season with four themed chapters—Working 9 to 5, Fun & Flirty, All Dressed Up and Change of Seasons. Whether you are dressing down or dressing up, whether you love long dangles or short hoops, and whatever the occasion—work, play, beach, holiday, wedding or just a night on the town— we have a design just for you.

Our helpful visual glossary of basic beading tools and supplies will help you figure out what you need to get started. The basic step-by-step instructions and full-colour photographs of every project take all the guesswork out of learning new techniques. We've also included a source listing with each set of instructions.

Once you're comfortable with beading earrings, try experimenting with different elements—size, colour, texture, materials or theme—and create a design all your own.

Hyacinth Honey, page 94

Many of our earring designs can be made—start to finish— in about half an hour. Others take a little more time, but it will be well worth it when you receive compliments and can tell your friends you made them yourself!

So, what are you waiting for? Check out all our enticing designs at a glance using the photo index on page 122, and decide which you'd like to create first. Bring out your beading stash, or get to the nearest craft store to stock up on fun and fabulous beading materials!

No matter what the occasion is, you'll always be dressed in style with beautiful earrings you've made yourself.

VISUAL GLOSSARY

Tools

Crimping pliers are used for just what their name implies —crimping! The back slot puts a seam in the middle of the crimp tube, separating the ends of the flex wire and trapping it firmly. The front slot rounds out the tube and turns it into a small, tidy bead.

Round-nose pliers are intended for turning round loops. They do not work well for holding or grasping since they tend to leave a small dent.

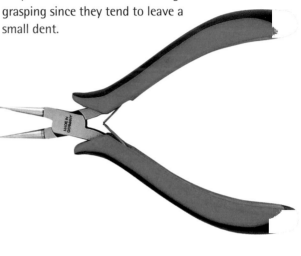

Chain-nose pliers are the most useful tool in your entire toolbox. They are used for holding, opening and closing jump rings and bending sharp angles.

Flat-nose pliers are a wire power tool. They are excellent for turning sharp corners, holding items and for opening and closing jump rings.

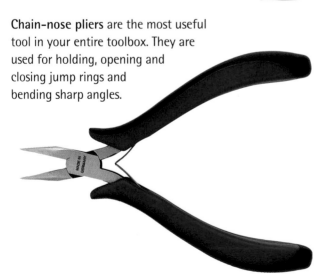

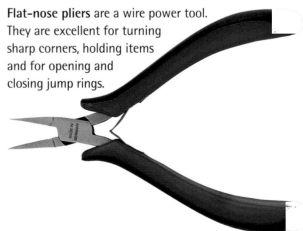

Wire flush cutters leave one flat side and one pointed side on each cut. Using flush cutters is especially important when working with heavy gauges of wire (20-gauge or smaller). One side of the cutter is flat, and the other is indented.

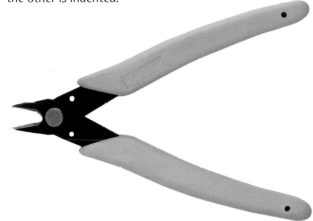

Nylon-jaw pliers can be used to harden or straighten wire.

Jeweller's hammers have fine, smooth curved heads that leave a clean impression. The round peen side works well for texturing wire and metal sheet.

A bench block is a flat, smooth piece of hardened steel. Hammering on top of a block flattens out and hardens the wire. Bench blocks are also used for stamping metal to get a clean impression.

Materials

Eye Pins are wires with a loop on one end and a straight portion of wire where beads can be strung. Length and gauges vary; most earrings use 24-gauge eye pins from 1½–2½ inches.

A head pin is a piece of wire with a stop end like a fine nail head. A bead slides onto the head pin and stops on the head. Lengths and gauges vary; most earrings use 24-gauge head pins from 1½–2½ inches.

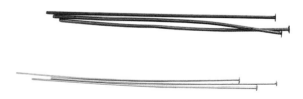

Jump rings are one of the most versatile findings used in jewellery making. They come in all sizes, gauges and metals. They are measured by diameter (width) and gauge (weight).

Ear wires come in many different styles. Regular fishhook style is the most common and the easiest to make yourself. Recommended weight for ear wires is either 22- or 20-gauge.

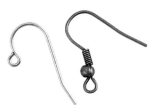

Crimp tubes are small, soft metal cylinders that can be flattened or formed around flexible beading wire to secure the ends. They are an essential component for bead-stringing projects.

Wire comes in many sizes or *gauges*. Gauge is the measured diameter of the wire. The higher the number, the thinner the wire. Wire can be tempered soft, half-hard or hard, which refers to its stiffness. Copper, silver and gold-filled are most commonly used for jewellery.

Flexible beading wire comes in several weights from .010–.026-inch diameter and is designed for stringing. It is available in precious metal and several colours and is made from 7 to 49 strands of steel wire, twisted and encased in a flexible plastic coating. Ends are finished with crimp beads using either crimping or chain-nose pliers.

BASICS STEP-BY-STEP

Opening & Closing Jump Rings

Jump rings are one of the most versatile findings used in jewellery making. They come in all sizes and gauges.

Use two pairs of smooth chain-nose pliers (bent or flat-nose pliers work fine as second pliers) (Photo A).

Photo A

Push ring open with right pliers while holding across the ring with left pliers. To close, hold in the same way and rock the ring back and forth until ring ends rub against

each other or you hear a click. Moving the ring past closed then back hardens the ring and assures a tight closure (Photo B).

Making an Eye Pin or Round Loop

Eye pins should be made with half-hard wire to make sure they hold their shape; 22-gauge will fit through most beads, with the exception of many semiprecious stones. Most Czech glass beads and 4mm crystals will fit on 20-gauge wire.

The length used for the eye loop depends on how big you want the loop. Here we will use ⅜ inch for a moderate-size loop.

Flush-trim end of wire (Photo C).

Photo C

Photo D

Photo B

Using chain-nose pliers, make a 90-degree bend ⅜ inch from end of wire (Photo D).

Using round-nose pliers, grasp the end of the wire so no wire sticks out between plier blades (Photo E).

Photo E

Begin making a loop by rolling your hand away from your body. Don't try to make the entire loop in one movement. Roll your hand a one-quarter turn counterclockwise (Photo F).

Photo F

Without removing pliers from loop, open plier blade slightly and pivot pliers back toward your body clockwise about a one-quarter turn (Photo G).

Photo G

Close pliers onto the wire and roll the loop until it comes around, next to the 90-degree bend (Photo H).

Photo H

Open and close eye-pin loops the same way as jump rings, by pushing open front to back (Photo I).

Photo I

Making Wire-Wrapped Loops

Practice wrapping wire with either 22- or 24-gauge wire. Harden slightly by pulling on one end with the other end clamped in a vise or pull one or two times through nylon-jaw pliers (Photo J).

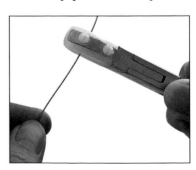

Photo J

Make a 90-degree bend about 1½ inches from end of the wire using chain-nose pliers (Photo K).

Photo K

Using round-nose pliers, grab wire about ⅜ inch away from the 90-degree and roll your hand away from yourself, toward the bend until a loop is halfway formed (Photos L and M).

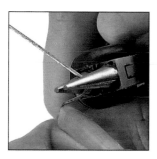

Photo L

Photo M

Without removing pliers from forming loop, open the jaw and rotate pliers clockwise about a one-quarter turn (Photo N).

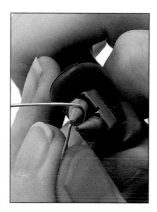

Photo N

Grab the end of the wire with your left (or non-dominant) hand and pull it around the rest of the way until it crosses itself and completes the loop (Photo O).

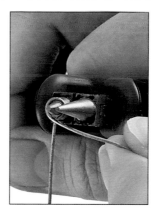

Photo O

Switch to chain-nose pliers, holding across the loop. Wrap tail around wire under loop with your left hand. If you are using a heavy gauge of wire, it is often easier to use a second pliers to pull the tail around instead of your fingers (Photos P and Q).

To create a wrap on the opposite end of the bead, leave a gap equal to wrap space on first end. Grasp to the right of the wrap space and make a 90-degree bend (Photos T and U).

Photo P

Photo T

Photo Q

Flush-cut wire as close to the wrap as possible. Tuck end down if needed, using chain-nose pliers (Photos R and S).

Photo R

Photo S

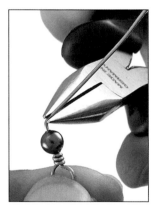

Photo U

Repeat steps from Photo L to Photo U to complete.

Hammering Wire

Hammering hardens and flattens round wire. This can be especially important when making ear wires or clasps that need to hold their shape. Always use a smooth, hardened steel surface to guarantee a clean finish. Any marks or scars on a bench block or hammer will impress on the surface of wire or sheet metal.

Create your shape from wire. Keep hammer flat to prevent marring the wire. Flip the wire over after a few taps and hammer on opposite side. Don't get carried away; if you hammer too much, metal becomes brittle and breaks (Photo V).

Photo V

Crimping

String a crimp bead onto flexible wire. String clasp or ring and pass tail of flexible wire back through crimp to form a loop.

Hold wires parallel and make sure crimp is positioned correctly. Using front slot on pliers, shape crimp into a small oval (Photo W).

Photo W

Put oval into back slot of pliers and squeeze to make fold in the centre with one wire on each side of fold (Photo X).

Photo X

Photo Y

Return to front slot, and squeeze again to tighten crimp. Do a few more rotations and squeezes to solidify and shape crimp bead. Trim wire tail (Photo Y).

CINDI

Breezy, with a sunny disposition and a flair for the dramatic, Cindi loves the basics. Cindi looks great with any outfit.

Design | Molly Schaller

Skill Level
Beginner

Finished Size
1½ inches long

Materials
2 (8mm) onyx round beads
2 (7mm) silver flower bead caps
2 (12mm) silver rings
2 (1-inch) silver eye pins
2 silver ear wires
Round-nose pliers
Chain-nose pliers
Flush cutters

Instructions

1) Slide an onyx round bead and a bead cap onto an eye pin. ***Note: String bead cap so it cups onyx bead.*** Form a loop; trim excess wire. Repeat once.

2) Open top loops of eye pins and attach to loops on ear wires; close loops.

3) Open bottom loops of eye pins and slide each onto silver rings; close loops. ∎

Cindi
Onyx beads, silver rings and ear wires from Fire Mountain Gems and Beads; bead caps from SHIANA.

KAIA'S DREAM

Simple ceramic and wooden beads balance perfectly with silver-plated discs. Dream on.

Design | Molly Schaller

Skill Level
Beginner

Finished Size
2 inches long

Materials
2 (8mm) Nangka wooden round beads
2 (20 x 20mm) sky blue ceramic Kazuri beads
2 (5mm) silver-plated discs
2 (2-inch) silver head pins
2 silver ear wires
Round-nose pliers
Chain-nose pliers
Flush cutters

Instructions
1) Onto one head pin, slide one silver disc, one Kazuri bead and one wooden round. Form a loop; trim excess wire.

2) Use chain-nose pliers to open loop and attach to ear wire; close loop.

3) Repeat steps 1 and 2 for second earring. ■

Kaia's Dream
Kazuri beads from Kazuri West; silver discs from Halcraft USA; wooden round beads from Fusion Beads; head pins from Beadalon.

GREEN WITH ENVY

Cast metal "slider" beads are lovely when paired with crystal bicones.

Design | Katie Hacker

Skill Level
Beginner

Finished Size
Approximately 1½ inches long

Materials
2 (12mm) green CRYSTALLIZED™ - Swarovski Elements round metal sliders with green inset crystals
4 (5mm) green CRYSTALLIZED™ - Swarovski Elements bicone crystals
2 (2-inch) silver head pins
2 silver ear wires
Round-nose pliers
Chain-nose pliers
Wire nippers

Instructions
1) String the following onto a head pin: green bicone crystal, round metal slider and another green bicone crystal.

2) Form a loop above top bead; trim off excess wire. Open loop and attach to an ear wire; close loop.

3) Repeat steps 1 and 2 for second earring. ■

FABRIC LOVE

Your Gram's tattered apron or that fabulous bag of retro quilting scraps—both are the perfect start to making these unique earrings.

Design | Candie Cooper

Skill Level
Easy

Finished Size
2 inches long

Materials
Printed fabric
Beads
2 silver flower spacer
   beads or brass
   flower charms
2 clear charms or tags
2 silver eye pins
2 jump rings
2 ear wires
Round-nose pliers
Chain-nose pliers
Wire nippers
Awl or large embroidery needle
Small foam brush
Decoupage medium

Instructions

1) Use charms as templates to cut two pieces from fabric.

2) Apply a layer of decoupage medium on back of a clear charm with foam brush. Press charm on top of one fabric piece and press down; burnish fabric on back so there are no air bubbles. Repeat once. Set aside to dry.

3) Use awl or large needle to poke a hole at centre top of each charm.

4) Open a jump ring and slide on a flower charm; slide jump ring through fabric charm. Close ring.

5) String a few beads on an eye pin; form a loop. Trim excess wire. Open one loop and attach to jump ring attached to charm; close loop.

6) Repeat steps 4 and 5 for second earring.

7) Open loops on ear wires and slide on top loops of dangles; close loops. ∎

Fabric Love

Clear glass square tags, jump rings and decoupage medium from Plaid Enterprises Inc.

HIDDEN SUN

Crystals float behind brass filigree windows, peeking out between delicate wires.

Design | Barb Switzer

Skill Level
Easy

Finished Size
1¾ inches long

Materials
2 (8mm) chili pepper CRYSTALLIZED™ - Swarovski
   Elements round crystals
2 (20 x 20mm) natural brass domed filigree squares
2 (22mm) natural brass hammered rings
2 (4.75mm) natural brass jump rings
2 (2-inch) 22-gauge natural brass head pins
2 natural brass ear wires
2 (5-link) sections 3mm natural brass cable chain
Round-nose pliers
2 pairs of chain-nose pliers
Flush cutters

Instructions
1) Slide a chili pepper crystal on a head pin; form a wrapped loop. Trim excess wire.

2) Use both pairs of chain-nose pliers to open end link of one 5-link chain; slide link onto ear-wire loop. Close link.

3) Open a jump ring and slide on the following: beaded head pin from step 1, hammered ring (textured side facing away from crystal), corner of a brass filigree square and end link of chain on ear wire. Close jump ring.

4) Repeat steps 1 to 3 for second earring. ∎

Hidden Sun
CRYSTALLIZED™ – Swarovski
Elements from INM Crystal Inc.;
head pins, chain, jump rings,
filigree squares, ear wires and
hammered brass rings from
Vintaj Natural Brass Co.

GARDEN LANTERN HOOPS

Semi-precious and polymer clay beads illuminate light, bright silver hoops. A perfect pair for an evening in the garden.

Design | Heather Powers

Skill Level
Easy

Finished Size
1¼ inches long

Materials
2 lime branch disc beads
12 (8mm) amazonite rondelles
12 nickel seed beads
14 (1-inch) sterling silver head pins
2 (4mm) silver spacers
2 (2mm) silver crimp beads
2 (25mm) sterling silver ear hoops
Round-nose pliers
Crimp pliers
Wire nippers

Instructions
1) Slide a spacer and a disc bead onto a head pin. Form a loop; trim excess wire. Repeat once.

2) Slide a seed bead and an amazonite rondelle onto a head pin. Form a loop; trim excess wire. Repeat 11 more times.

3) String three amazonite dangles, disc bead dangle and three amazonite dangles onto one hoop. Repeat once.

4) String one crimp bead onto very end of one hoop; use crimp pliers to squeeze gently on crimp bead to create a stopper.

5) Repeat steps 1 to 4 for second earring. ■

Garden Lantern Hoops
Branch disc beads from
Humblebeads; seed beads
from Charlene's Beads.

RED DOUGHNUTS

Turn drilled doughnuts or loops into dangle earrings.

Design | Laurie D'Ambrosio

Skill Level
Easy

Finished Size
1¾ inches long

Materials
2 (14mm) red drilled doughnuts
2 (6mm) black round beads
2 gold head pins
2 (1¼-inch) lengths
　20-gauge gold wire
2 gold ear wires
Round-nose pliers
Wire nippers

Instructions
1) Beginning from inside a red doughnut, thread head pin up through one hole. *Note: The head pin will need to be curved slightly to fit into hole.* Form a loop at top of bead; trim excess wire.

2) Form a loop at one end of one 1¼-inch wire; string round bead. Form another loop; trim excess wire.

3) Open one loop on bead link and attach to red doughnut head pin; close loop. Open opposite loop and attach to ear wire; close loop.

4) Repeat steps 1 to 3 for second earring. ■

Red Doughnuts

Red doughnuts from Blue
Moon Beads; black beads
from Halcraft USA.

ALL WRAPPED UP

Ribbon adds vibrant colour as well as texture to these earrings you can wrap up in no time.

Design | Brenda Morris Jarrett

Skill Level
Easy

Finished Size
3¼–3½ inches long

Materials
2 (38-inch) lengths ⅜-inch-wide ribbon
   yarn in desired colour
Silver or gold jump rings: 2 (9mm), 2 (12mm)
2 round or oval resin hoop earrings minus
   wires and jump rings
2 silver ear wires
Soft cloth
Chain-nose pliers
White all-purpose glue

Instructions
1) Clean and dry resin earrings with soft cloth.

2) Apply glue to both sides of one earring and use your fingers to spread glue on both sides and edges.

3) Beginning at top of hoop, start wrapping a 38-inch length of ribbon yarn around hoop, overlapping each wrap slightly, covering edges. Pull ribbon tight as it is being wrapped, but not tight enough that it puckers. Ribbon should be snug around edges. Use a water-dampened finger to apply additional glue to hoop as needed to secure ribbon.

4) When entire hoop is covered, cut ribbon on reverse side of hoop so it covers beginning ribbon end. Apply a small amount of glue to ribbon end and press to secure. Use wet finger to smooth ribbon along entire hoop. Let dry thoroughly.

5) Repeat steps 2 to 4 for other hoop.

6) Open a 12mm jump ring and attach it to centre top of hoop; attach ring to a 9mm jump ring. Close ring. Open 9mm jump ring and attach to ear wire; close ring. Repeat for other hoop. ■

All Wrapped Up
Incredible ribbon yarn
from Lion Brand Yarn Co.

LHASA DROPS

Inspired by the beauty of traditional Tibetan jewellery, this pair of earrings uses the time-honoured combination of turquoise, coral and sterling silver.

Design | Rupa Balachandar

Skill Level
Easy

Finished Size
3 inches long

Materials
2 (10 x 35mm) sterling silver tubular beads
Reconstituted turquoise round beads:
   2 (10mm), 2 (4mm)
2 (5mm) red coral round beads
2 (1-inch) silver head pins
2 (2½-inch) silver eye pins
2 sterling silver French ear wires
Round-nose pliers
Chain-nose pliers
Wire nippers

Instructions

1) Slide a coral bead and a 10mm turquoise bead on a head pin. Form a loop; trim excess wire.

2) Open loop and attach to loop on an eye pin; close loop. Slide a silver tubular bead onto eye pin along with a 4mm turquoise bead. Form a loop; trim excess wire.

3) Open loop and slide onto loop on ear wire; close loop.

4) Repeat steps 1 to 3 for second earring. ■

Lhasa Drops
Beads and ear wires
from RupaB Designs.

IN THE LOOP

Use circular links and jump rings to make a swinging fashion statement. This design will also work with shell rings, "O" rings and small doughnuts.

Design | Laurie D'Ambrosio

Skill Level
Easy

Finished Size
2¼ inches long

Materials
2 (29mm) turquoise rings
6 (5mm) turquoise bugle beads
14 (10mm) silver jump rings
6 (1-inch) silver head pins
2 (2-inch) silver eye pins
2 silver fishhook ear wires
Round-nose pliers
Chain-nose pliers
Wire nippers

Instructions

1) Hold one eye pin up against reverse side of a turquoise ring with loop pointing upward. Bend wire below loop around ring, forming a large loop, securing eye pin to ring. Trim excess wire. Open loop on ear wire and attach to original eye-pin loop; close loop.

2) Open and attach seven jump rings onto turquoise ring; close rings.

3) Slide a bugle bead onto a head pin. Form a loop; trim excess wire. Repeat two more times.

4) Open loops on beaded head pins. Attach one to centre jump ring; skip one jump ring on each side of centre jump ring and attach remaining beaded head pins.

5) Repeat steps 1 to 4 for second earring. ∎

In the Loop
Turquoise rings from Plaid Enterprises
Inc.; bugle beads from Blue Moon Beads;
findings from Hirschberg Schutz & Co. Inc.

LUXE LOTUS

Often referred to as the rose of the East, the lotus symbolizes purity and elegance in a feminine form.

Design | Molly Schaller

Skill Level
Beginner

Finished Size
1¾ inches long

Materials
2 (8mm) bronze CRYSTALLIZED™ - Swarovski
   Elements crystal pearls
2 (16mm) silver white Thai Karen Hill Tribe
   lotus leaf charms
2 (1-inch) sterling silver eye pins
2 sterling silver ear wires
Round-nose pliers
Chain-nose pliers
Flush cutters

Instructions
1) Slide a pearl on an eye pin; form a loop. Trim excess wire.

2) Open loop and slide on leaf charm; close loop.

3) Open opposite loop of eye pin and slide it onto ear-wire loop; close loop.

4) Repeat steps 1 to 3 for second earring. ■

Luxe Lotus
Ear wires and eye pins from Fire Mountain Gems and Beads; lotus leaf charms from SHIANA; pearls from CRYSTZALLIZED™ – Swarovski Elements.

HOOPLA

These hoop earrings create a visual treat because of the alternating drops of turquoise and coral beads. They will add pizzazz to any outfit.

Design | Rupa Balachandar

Skill Level
Easy

Finished Size
2¾ inches long

Materials
4–5mm round beads: 18 coral,
    18 reconstituted turquoise
18 (1-inch) gold head pins
2 (55mm) gold-filled 9-loop ear hoops
Round-nose pliers
Chain-nose pliers
Wire nippers

Instructions
1) Slide a coral bead and a turquoise bead on a head pin. Form a loop; trim excess wire. Repeat nine more times for a total of 10 dangles. These will be referred to as A dangles.

2) Slide a turquoise bead and a coral bead on a head pin. Form a loop; trim excess wire. Repeat seven more times for a total of eight dangles. These will be referred to as B dangles.

3) Open loop on an A dangle and attach to first loop on an ear hoop; close loop. Open loop on a B dangle and attach to second loop on ear hoop; close loop. Continue attaching dangles to ear hoop, alternating A and B dangles until all loops are filled.

4) Repeat step 3 to complete second earring. ■

Hoopla
Beads and ear hoops from RupaB Designs.

MAN IN THE MOON

If you ever wondered if the moon was truly made of green cheese, allow this pair of earrings to whisper the secret answer right in your ears!

Design | Jean Yates

Skill Level
Easy

Finished Size
Approximately 2¾ inches long

Materials
2 seafoam blossom oval links
2 black-and-white Charlie Moon pendants
2 (6mm) erinite CRYSTALLIZED™ - Swarovski Elements
    bicone crystals
2 (4–5mm) oxidized sterling silver daisy spacers
2 (3.5mm) sterling silver hexagonal beads
2 (3-inch) 22-gauge sterling silver head pins
2 (6mm) sterling silver snap-close jump rings
2 sterling silver ear wires
Round-nose pliers
2 pairs chain-nose pliers
Wire nippers

Instructions

1) Slide a hexagonal bead, daisy spacer and an erinite bicone onto a head pin; form a wrapped loop, attaching loop to top loop of moon pendant before wrapping. Trim excess wire. *Note: Keep cut end of wrapped loop on back of wire.*

2) Using both pairs of chain-nose pliers, open a jump ring and attach it to moon pendant, making sure beaded head pin hangs to the left of the jump ring. Slide oval link onto jump ring before closing.

3) Slide opposite loop of oval link onto ear wire.

4) Repeat steps 1 to 3 for second earring. ■

Man in the Moon

Oval links and moon pendants from
Earthenwood Studio; bicone crystals from
Fusion Beads; hexagonal beads, head pins
and ear wires from The Bead Shop; snap-
close jump rings from Via Murano.

BRASS PETAL DROPS

Nostalgic and sweet, crystal pearls in rose and verdant hues dangle between brass links for earrings that are reminiscent of cool spring mornings, fresh with dew.

Design | Molly Schaller

Skill Level
Easy

Finished Size
2¼ inches long

Materials
CRYSTALLIZED™ - Swarovski
  Elements round pearls: 2 (3mm)
  pink, 2 (4mm) mauve, 2 (6mm)
  light green
2 (11 x 8mm) cream
  CRYSTALLIZED™ - Swarovski
  Elements teardrop pearls
2 (8mm) brass foliage bead caps
6 (1-inch) brass eye pins
2 (1-inch) brass head pins
2 brass ear wires
Round-nose pliers
Chain-nose pliers
Wire nippers

Instructions
1) Using round-nose pliers, turn tips of petals on bead caps upward slightly.

2) Slide one round pearl onto each eye pin. Form a loop on each eye pin; trim excess wire. There should be a total of six pearl links.

3) Slide one teardrop pearl and one bead cap onto each head pin. *Note: String bead caps so they cup narrow end of teardrop pearls.* Form a loop on each head pin; trim excess wire.

4) Open and close loops to attach pearl links to one ear wire in the following order from top to bottom: 3mm pearl link, 4mm pearl link, 5mm pearl link and teardrop pearl dangle.

5) Repeat step 4 to assemble second earring. ∎

Brass Petal Drops

Pearls from CRYSTALLIZED™ – Swarovski Elements; ear wires, eye pins, head pins and bead caps from Vintaj Natural Brass Co.

SHERBET SWIRLS

Pretty shades of pink swirl and twist in these memory wire earrings that look good enough to eat.

Design | Sandy Parpart

Skill Level
Intermediate

Finished Size
3 inches long

Materials
Pink Czech glass mini bead mix (includes pink seed beads, pink E beads, and white and clear bugle beads)
6 (2-inch) silver head pins
Silver jump rings: 2 (4mm), 2 (7mm)
2 silver ear wires
Bracelet memory wire
Round-nose pliers
Chain-nose pliers
Heavy-duty wire cutters or memory wire shears

Note
Memory wire is hard to cut and will damage regular wire nippers. Always use memory wire shears to cut wire coils.

Instructions
1) Cut one coil, plus ½ inch from memory wire. Using round-nose pliers and referring to Figure 1, form a loop at one end of wire. *Note: Forming loops on memory wire may take some time as it is difficult to do due to the strength of the wire.*

2) String a mix of beads onto memory wire; this can be done in a pattern or randomly.

3) Referring to Figure 1, form another loop at end of wire. If needed, trim excess wire.

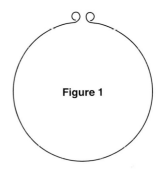

Figure 1

4) Slide 1 inch of assorted beads onto a head pin; form a wrapped head-pin loop above top bead. Set aside. Repeat twice more.

5) Open a 7mm jump ring and slide on beaded head pins; attach jump ring through both loops on beaded memory wire, forming a hoop. Close jump ring. Beaded head pins should dangle through centre of hoop.

6) Open a 4mm jump ring and slide on assembled hoop; attach jump ring to ear wire. Close jump ring.

7) Repeat steps 1 to 6 for second earring. ■

Sherbet Swirls
Beads from Blue Moon Beads.

DEWDROPS

Form a wire leaf shape and accent it with earth-toned freshwater pearl dangles.

Design | Amy Cornwell

Skill Level
Intermediate

Finished Size
2¼ inches long

Materials
5–6mm freshwater pearls:
  2 white, 2 blue,
  2 pale green,
  2 cream, 2 pink
2 (6mm) gold-filled round beads
10 (2-inch) gold-filled head pins
2 gold-filled ear wires
10 inches 21-gauge gold-filled wire
Ring mandrel
Round-nose pliers
Flat-nose pliers
Wire nippers

Instructions
1) Slide a pearl on a head pin; form a wrapped head-pin loop above pearl. Trim excess wire. Repeat for each pearl.

2) Cut two 3½-inch lengths of wire. Set remaining wire aside. Use flat-nose pliers to gently bend one wire into a 90-degree angle at centre (Figure 1). Wrap wire around large portion of ring mandrel to form a leaf shape (Figure 2). Repeat for second wire.

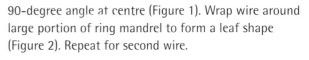

Figure 1   **Figure 2**

3) String five pearl head pins on each leaf, one of each colour.

4) Form a small loop at both ends of each leaf, positioning loops so they are both facing inward. *Note: The leaf may need to be wrapped around mandrel again to get wire ends to meet.*

5) Cut remaining wire into two 1½-inch lengths. Form a wrapped loop ½ inch from one end of one wire, attaching loop to both loops on one wire leaf before wrapping. String a gold-filled round bead and form another wrapped loop. Trim excess wire. Repeat for second earring.

6) Open loops on ear wires and slide on wrapped loops; close loops. ∎

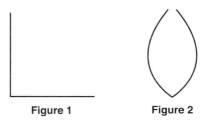

SASSY SEQUIN HOOPS

These sassy earrings are easy to make and perfect for people of just about every age. Lightweight, a little sparkly and all fun!

Design | Alexa Westerfield

Skill Level
Beginner

Finished Size
2¼ inches long

Materials
Sequin beaded fringe with 4 different sizes of sequins
12 (4mm) silver-plated round beads
2 silver hoops
2 silver-plated ear wires
Chain-nose pliers

Instructions
1) Cut off two large sequins, four medium sequins, four small sequins and four tiny sequins from fringe.

2) String the following on a hoop, stringing a silver bead between each: tiny sequin, small sequin, medium sequin, large sequin, medium sequin, small sequin and tiny sequin.

3) Using pliers, bend back end of hoop approximately ⅛ inch. Insert end into hoop to close.

4) Open loop on ear wire and slide on loop on hoop; close loop.

5) Repeat steps 2 to 4 for second earring. ■

Sassy Sequin Hoops
Sequin fringe from Wal-Mart Stores Inc.; silver-plated beads, hoops and ear wires from Michaels Stores Inc.

SWING IT, SISTER

Sparkly, swingy earrings are sure to get attention, especially with your hair swept up in a 60s-style beehive.

Design | Margot Potter

Skill Level
Easy

Finished Size
3½ inches long

Materials
CRYSTALLIZED™ - Swarovski Elements briolettes:
    8 (12 x 6.5mm) erinite, 8 (11 x 5.5mm) light
    Colorado topaz, 8 (11 x 5.5mm) light rose
Open-centre Quick Links circles: 4 (12mm), 2 (25mm)
28 (5mm) silver-plated jump rings
2 silver-plated large kidney ear wires
2 pairs of chain-nose pliers

Note
Use both pairs of chain-nose pliers to open jump rings.

Instructions
1) Attach a jump ring to each briolette. Set aside.

2) Attach circles together as follows with jump rings: 12mm, 12mm and 25mm.

3) Slide first 12mm circle onto ear wire. Use pliers to gently squeeze ear wire around circle so it is stationary.

4) Slide a light rose briolette, erinite briolette and a light Colorado topaz briolette onto 25mm circle. Repeat three more times.

5) Repeat steps 2 to 4 for second earring. *Note: Slide briolettes on second earring in opposite direction so second earring is a mirror of first earring.*

6) Check back through to ensure jump rings are properly closed. ■

Swing It, Sister
Briolettes from CRYSTALLIZED™ -
Swarovski Elements; Quick Links
and findings from Beadalon.

FEELIN' THE BLUES

These blue beauties are perfect for dressing up with a fancy top or dressing down with your favourite jeans.

Design | Alexa Westerfield

Skill Level
Beginner

Finished Size
2¾ inches long

Materials
2 (16mm) light blue transparent disc beads
4 (4mm) blue cat's-eye beads
4 (4mm) silver-plated daisy spacers
2 silver-plated head pins
2 (1-inch) pieces silver chain
Round-nose pliers
Wire nippers

Instructions
1) String the following on a head pin: cat's-eye bead, spacer, disc, spacer and cat's-eye bead. Form a loop; attach loop to end link of one 1-inch chain before closing. Trim excess wire. Repeat once.

2) Open loops on ear wires and attach to end links of chains; close loops. ■

Feelin' the Blues
Light blue disc beads, spacers and chain from Michaels Stores Inc.; blue cat's-eye beads from Darice Inc.

COPPER CRAZE

Copper and sterling are a classic and stunning combination. Learn to hammer wire to give it strength and texture, plus get some practice at spirals—a wire jewellery fundamental.

Design | Laura McIvor

Skill Level
Intermediate

Finished Size
2½ inches long

Materials
Wire: 12 inches 20-gauge sterling silver, 10 inches 18-gauge sterling silver, 10 inches 18-gauge copper

Copper round beads: 4 (4mm), 2 (8mm)

4 (5mm) silver daisy spacers

2 (5mm) 16-gauge silver jump rings

2 silver ear wires

Round-nose pliers

Chain-nose pliers

Wire nippers

Planishing hammer

Small anvil

Instructions
1) Cut a 6-inch piece of 20-gauge sterling silver wire. Form a wrapped loop at one end. String the following: 4mm copper bead, daisy spacer, 8mm copper bead, daisy spacer and a 4mm copper bead. Form a wrapped loop; trim excess wire.

2) Cut a 5-inch piece of 18-gauge sterling silver wire. Form a spiral at one end, leaving a ½-inch tail. Form a small loop at end of ½-inch tail. Referring to photo, use chain-nose pliers to twist small loop 90 degrees.

3) Use small anvil and planishing hammer to flatten and harden the spiral. Hammer small loop to harden wire and provide added strength.

4) Repeat steps 2 and 3 with copper wire.

5) Open a jump ring and slide on sterling silver and copper dangles; slide jump ring onto beaded wire from step 1 before closing.

6) Open loop on ear wire and attach to opposite end of beaded wire; close loop.

7) Repeat steps 1 to 6 for second earring. ∎

Copper Craze
Copper beads from
Capilano Rock & Gem.

CRYSTAL STASH

These tiny glass vials hold a small stash of crystal beads to make a whimsical yet elegant effect. It's easy to switch up the beads on the inside if your mood or your outfit changes.

Design | Margot Potter

Skill Level
Easy

Finished Size
2 inches long

Materials
3mm CRYSTALLIZED™ - Swarovski Elements round
    crystals: 10 jet, 12 light rose AB, 10 crystal vitrial AB
2 (1½-inch) clear test-tube glass vials
2 (4mm) gold-plated jump rings
6 gold-plated head pins
2 gold-plated ear wires
Round-nose pliers
2 pairs of chain-nose pliers
Wire nippers
Jeweller's glue (optional)

Instructions
1) Fill vials with four jet crystals, four crystal vitrial AB crystals and five light rose AB crystals, alternating colours as you fill. Seal vial, using glue to permanently seal vial if desired.

2) Slide a crystal on a head pin; form a wrapped loop. Trim excess wire. Repeat for each remaining crystal for a total of six beaded dangles.

3) Open a jump ring and slide on one of each colour of dangle; close ring. Repeat once.

4) Open loop at top of vial using chain-nose pliers. Slide beaded jump ring and ear wire on loop; close loop. Repeat once.

5) Turn eyes of ear wires so earrings are facing forward using chain-nose pliers to adjust. ■

Crystal Stash
Glass vials from ARTchix Studio; crystals from CRYSTALLIZED™ – Swarovski Elements; findings from Beadalon.

WARM BRONZE PEARL CHANDELIERS

Dream an evening of elegance to go with soft gold and glowing pearls. Classic chandelier findings meet their perfect match.

Design | Sandy Parpart

Skill Level
Intermediate

Finished Size
3 inches long

Materials
CRYSTALLIZED™ - Swarovski Elements crystal pearls:
  8 (6mm) bronze, 6 (5mm) brown
22 (4mm) silk CRYSTALLIZED™ - Swarovski Elements
  bicone crystals
8 (1½-inch) gold-plated head pins
8 (5mm) gold-plated jump rings
2 (3-into-1) gold chandelier components
2 gold lever-back ear wires
Round-nose pliers
Needle-nose pliers
Wire nippers

Instructions
1) Slide the following onto a head pin: bronze pearl and two silk crystals. Form a wrapped loop; trim excess wire. Attach a jump ring to wrapped loop and attach to top loop on chandelier component.

2) Slide the following onto a head pin: silk crystal, brown pearl, silk crystal, bronze pearl and a silk crystal. Form a wrapped loop; trim excess wire. Attach a jump ring to wrapped loop. Repeat two more times.

3) Open jump rings and attach to bottom loops on chandelier component; close loop.

4) Repeat steps 1 to 3 for second earring. ■

Warm Bronze Pearl Chandeliers
CRYSTALLIZED™ - Swarovski Elements
crystals and pearls from Fusion Beads;
chandelier components and ear wires
from Hirschberg Schutz & Co. Inc.

DANGLING BY A THREAD

Make elegant earrings in a snap with a few small lightweight beads. Change the length of the earring by pulling more of the chain through to the back.

Design | Laurie D'Ambrosio

Skill Level
Easy

Finished Size
3¼ inches long

Materials
4 (4mm) crystal AB CRYSTALLIZED™ - Swarovski Elements bicone crystals
Round beads: 2 (6mm) fuchsia, 4 (4mm) black
6 (1-inch) sterling silver head pins
2 sterling silver ear threads
Round-nose pliers
Chain-nose pliers
Wire nippers

Instructions
1) Slide a black round, fuchsia round and a black round on a head pin. Form a loop; trim excess wire. Repeat once.

2) Slide a crystal AB bicone on a head pin. Form a loop; trim excess wire. Repeat three more times.

3) Open loops on two crystal AB dangles and attach to loop on an ear thread; close loops. Open loop on one black/fuchsia dangle and slide onto one of the crystal AB dangle loops attached to ear thread. Close loop.

4) Repeat step 3 for second earring. ■

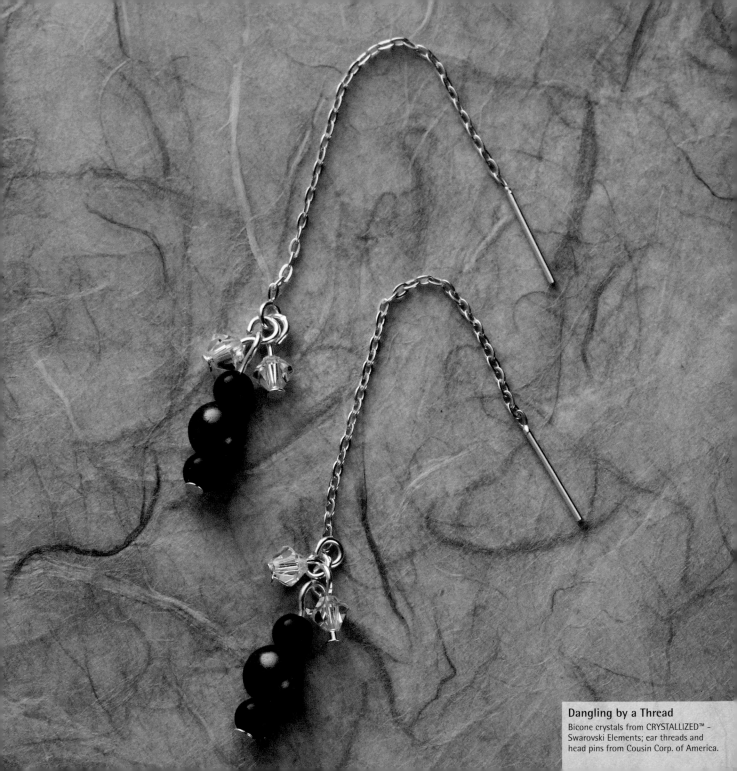

Dangling by a Thread
Bicone crystals from CRYSTALLIZED™ –
Swarovski Elements; ear threads and
head pins from Cousin Corp. of America.

DOTS & STRIPES ON DISPLAY

Yellow and black are the perfect colours to wear when you want to stand out in the crowd.

Design | Alexa Westerfield

Skill Level
Easy

Finished Size
2¼ inches long

Materials
2 yellow and black polka-dot ceramic round beads
   with shank
2 (11mm) black-and-white striped acrylic cylinder beads
4 (6/0) yellow seed beads
2 silver-plated eye pins
2 (10mm) silver jump rings
2 silver-plated ear wires
Round-nose pliers
Chain-nose pliers
Wire nippers

Instructions

1) Open a jump ring and slide on one polka-dot bead; close ring.

2) Slide a yellow seed bead, black-and-white striped bead and a yellow seed bead on an eye pin. Form a loop; trim excess wire.

3) Open bottom loop of eye pin and slide on jump ring from step 1. Close loop.

4) Open ear-wire loop and attach to top loop of beaded eye pin; close loop.

5) Repeat steps 1 to 4 for second earring. ■

Dots & Stripes on Display
Polka-dot beads from Creative Impressions in Clay; seed beads, jump rings and ear wires from Jo-Ann Stores Inc.

WHEN THE SHARK BITES

These art bead earrings balance a variety of colours. What more could you ask from such an unusual mix of metals and crystal?

Design | Jean Yates

Skill Level
Easy

Finished Size
3 inches long

Materials
2 shark bottlecap beads
40 antique brass heishi spacers
4 (8mm) jet AB CRYSTALLIZED™ - Swarovski
   Elements cubes
2 (3-inch) 24-gauge gold-filled head pins
2 (6mm) gold-filled snap-close jump rings
2 gold-filled ear wires
Round-nose pliers
2 pairs of chain-nose pliers
Wire nippers

Instructions

1) String the following onto a head pin: five heishi spacers, jet AB cube, five heishi spacers, shark bead, five heishi spacers, jet AB cube and five heishi spacers. Form a wrapped loop; trim excess wire. Repeat once, stringing shark bead so shark faces opposite direction.

2) Use jump rings to attach beaded dangles to ear wires, using both pairs of chain-nose pliers to open jump rings.

3) Repeat steps 1 and 2 for second earring. ■

When the Shark Bites
Bottlecap beads from Glass Garden Beads; heishi spacers from Objects and Elements; CRYSTALLIZED™ - Swarovski Elements cubes from Fusion Beads; snap-close jump rings from Via Murano.

OCEANS OF DELIGHT

These flirty earrings will be your "go to" summertime pair. Freshwater pearls, apatite and rutilated quartz cascade from sterling hoops for an enchanting effect.

Design | Margot Potter

Skill Level
Intermediate

Finished Size
1⅛ inches long

Materials
8 (8mm) freeform apatite nuggets
8 (6mm) cream freshwater pearls
8 (8mm) rutilated quartz coins
24 (24-gauge) sterling silver head pins
4 (2 x 2mm) sterling silver crimp tubes
2 (1¼-inch) sterling silver hoops
Round-nose pliers
2 pairs chain-nose pliers
Wire nippers

Instructions
1) String a crimp tube onto hoop and slide it up against receptive end of hoop. Use chain-nose pliers to flatten and secure tube in place with chain-nose pliers. This will prevent beaded dangles from falling off. Repeat for second hoop.

2) Slide a bead onto a head pin; form a wrapped loop. Trim excess wire. Repeat for each head pin.

3) Slide beaded dangles onto hoop as follows: pearl, rutilated quartz and apatite. Repeat three more times; slide on a pearl and rutilated quartz. Repeat for second earring.

4) Flatten and secure a crimp tube approximately ⅛ inch from insertion end of hoop. Repeat for second earring.

5) Use round-pliers to bend wire end on each hoop up at a 90-degree angle to secure earrings closed when wearing. ■

Oceans of Delight
Apatite nuggets from Bead Trust;
freshwater pearls and rutilated quartz
coins from Wonder Sources Inc.; findings
from Marvin Schwab/The Bead Warehouse.

TRIUMVIRATE

Dramatic, textured ear wires and royal green drops make a simple earring look like expensive jewellery from a glass case.

Design | Barb Switzer

Skill Level
Easy

Finished Size
2 inches long

Materials
Palace green CRYSTALLIZED™ -
  Swarovski Elements briolettes:
  4 (11 x 5.5mm), 2 (13 x 6.5mm)
Sterling silver jump rings:
  6 (4mm), 2 (5mm)
2 (44 x 20mm) silver textured ear wires
1 inch sterling silver flat oval link chain
2 pairs chain-nose pliers
Flush cutters

Instructions

1) Cut two pieces of chain, each three links long.

2) Use both pairs of pliers to open a 4mm jump ring; slide ring onto end link of one chain and attach to ear-wire loop. Close ring.

3) Use a 5mm jump ring to attach large briolette to end link of chain.

4) Use a 4mm jump ring to attach a smaller briolette to centre link of chain. Repeat on opposite side of same chain link.

5) Repeat steps 2 to 4 for second earring. ■

Triumvirate
All materials from Fusion Beads.

PURPLE PASSION DROPS

You will love that these earrings are sophisticated and glamorous at the same time! The purple lucite jewels make a glitzy and playful statement.

Design | Alexa Westerfield

Skill Level
Easy

Finished Size
3 inches long

Materials
2 (22 x 18mm) lavender acrylic faceted top-drilled beads
6 (6mm) purple glass pearls
Silver jump rings: 6 (15mm), 2 (8mm)
6 silver-plated head pins
2 silver-plated ear wires
Round-nose pliers
2 pairs of chain-nose pliers
Wire nippers

Note
Use both pairs of chain-nose pliers to open jump rings.

Instructions
1) Slide a pearl onto a head pin; form a loop. Trim excess wire. Repeat for each pearl.

2) Open one 15mm jump ring and slide on two more 15mm jump rings; close ring.

3) Open 8mm jump ring and attach to light purple faceted bead; slide jump ring onto one of the end jump rings from step 2. Close ring.

4) Open loop on a pearl head pin and attach it around both the first and second 15mm jump rings; close loop. Repeat to attach a second pearl head pin around second and third 15mm jump rings. Attach another pearl head pin to top 15mm jump ring.

5) Open loop on ear wire and attach to top 15mm jump ring and pearl head pin; close loop.

6) Repeat steps 2 to 5 for second earring. ■

Purple Passion Drops
Top-drilled beads from Hobby Lobby Stores Inc.; glass pearls from Wal-Mart Stores Inc.

CLEOPATRA

Cleopatra makes a statement. Marquis-cut onyx hangs from gold-filled chain accented with iolite, onyx and labradorite stones.

Design | Molly Schaller

Skill Level
Intermediate

Finished Size
3¼ inches long

Materials
6 (2mm) black onyx round beads
4 (3mm) iolite rondelles
2 (4mm) labradorite rondelles
2 (12 x 8mm) black onyx top-drilled marquise beads
4 (1-inch) gold eye pins
6 inches gold figure-8 chain
10 inches 26-gauge dead-soft gold-filled wire
2 gold ear wires
Round-nose pliers
Chain-nose pliers
Flush cutters

Instructions
1) Cut chain into the following lengths: two 2-inch pieces and two 1-inch pieces. Cut wire into two 5-inch pieces.

2) String the following onto an eye pin: black onyx round, iolite rondelle, labradorite rondelle, iolite rondelle and black onyx round. Form a loop; trim excess wire.

3) Slide one black onyx round onto an eye pin. Form a loop and trim excess wire.

4) String a black onyx marquise onto centre of a 5-inch wire. Bring both wire ends above centre top of bead. Wrap one wire around other wire just above bead; form a small wrapped loop with other wire, attaching loop to centre link of a 2-inch chain before wrapping. Trim excess wire.

5) Open one loop of beaded eye pin from step 2 and attach to end link of 2-inch chain with attached bead. Slide end link of one 1-inch chain onto loop before closing.

6) Open opposite loop of beaded eye pin and attach to opposite ends of 2-inch and 1-inch chains, making sure chains are not twisted.

7) Open one loop of beaded eye pin from step 3 and slide it onto centre link of 1-inch chain; close loop. Open opposite loop and attach to loop of ear wire. Close loop.

8) Repeat steps 2 to 7 for second earring. ∎

QUEEN FOR A DAY

Crystals and pearls make columns of sparkle suitable for a blushing bride.

Design | Molly Schaller

Skill Level
Intermediate

Finished Size
2¾ inches long

Materials
16 (5mm) peach CRYSTALLIZED™ - Swarovski Elements crystal pearls
CRYSTALLIZED™ - Swarovski Elements AB round crystals: 18 (3mm), 2 (6mm)
2 (10mm) crystal AB CRYSTALLIZED™ - Swarovski Elements gold flower charms
16 (4mm) gold-plated scalloped bead caps
Gold head pins: 4 (2-inch), 4 (1-inch)
Gold eye pins: 2 (2-inch), 2 (1-inch)
4 (15mm) 3-hole gold spacer bars
2 gold French hook ear wires
Round-nose pliers
Chain-nose pliers
Flush cutters

Instructions
1) Onto one 1-inch eye pin, slide the following: bead cap, 6mm crystal and a bead cap, with bead caps cupping crystal. Form a loop after bead cap; trim excess wire. Set aside.

2) Onto one 1-inch head pin, slide one pearl. Form a loop after pearl; trim excess wire. Repeat once. Set aside pearl dangles.

3) Onto one 2-inch head pin, slide one 3mm crystal; insert head pin through an outer hole on a spacer bar. Slide the following onto the head pin: pearl, bead cap (bead caps should cup pearls), 3mm crystal, bead cap, pearl, outer hole on a second spacer bar and a 3mm crystal. Form a loop; trim excess wire.

4) Repeat step 3 with another 2-inch head pin for opposite outer hole of spacer bar.

5) Repeat step 3 with a 2-inch eye pin using centre hole of spacer bar.

6) Open loops on pearl dangles and attach to outer loops at bottom of earring using chain-nose pliers to open and close loops. Open centre bottom loop and slide on gold flower charm; close loop.

7) Attach crystal link from step 1 to top centre loop of earring. Open ear wire loop and attach to top loop of crystal link; close loop.

8) Repeat steps 1 to 7 for a second earring. ■

Queen for a Day

Crystals and pearls from CRYSTALLIZED™ - Swarovski Elements; bead caps and spacer bars from Fusion Beads; head pins and eye pins from Beadalon.

LOOPY SILVER BEADS

These funky, loopy, wrapped silver wire beads make an unusual pair of earrings. Four beads and a few findings make a truly unique design.

Design | Carole Rodgers

Skill Level
Easy

Finished Size
2½ inches long

Materials
Silver round loopy wire beads: 2 (20mm), 2 (12mm)
8 (3.5mm) silver round beads
4 (2-inch) silver ball-tip head pins
6 (4mm) silver jump rings
2 silver ear wires
Fine silver chain: 2 (3-link) pieces, 2 (9-link) pieces
Round-nose pliers
Chain-nose pliers
Flush cutters

Instructions

1) String a silver round bead, loopy wire bead and a silver round bead on a head pin; form a wrapped loop. Trim excess wire. Repeat for each loopy wire bead.

2) Use jump rings to attach one end of 3-link chains to small loopy wire beaded head pins and one end of 9-link chains to large loopy wire beaded head pins.

3) Open a jump ring and slide on end links of two chains, one of each size; attach jump ring to loop on ear wire. Close jump ring. Repeat for second earring.

4) Repeat steps 1 to 3 for second earring. ■

Loopy Silver Beads
Loopy wire beads from Oriental
Trading Co.; findings from Beadalon.

FORBIDDEN CITY

Bold colours and beautiful textures, inspired by one of China's ancient places, make a stunning design.

Design | Candie Cooper

Skill Level
Intermediate

Finished Size
2½ inches long

Materials
Siam CRYSTALLIZED™ -
   Swarovski Elements bicone
   crystals: 20 (3mm), 2 (5mm)
2 (12mm) cloisonné beads
2 (24.8 x 16.4mm) 3-to-1 gold
   chandelier components
4 (4mm) gold jump rings
2 gold ball- and star-tipped head pins
2 gold ear wires
10 inches 3mm gold link chain
20 inches 24-gauge gold wire
Round-nose pliers
Chain-nose pliers
Wire nippers

Instructions
1) Cut 20 (1-inch) pieces of gold wire. Form a small loop at end of each wire. String a 3mm Siam bicone on each wire and finish with a small loop, positioning loops so they are perpendicular to each other. Trim excess wire.

2) Divide crystal links into two groups of 10. Open one loop and connect it to the next; close loop. Continue in the same manner to make a beaded chain consisting of 10 links. Repeat for remaining links.

3) Cut two 2¾-inch pieces and two 2¼-inch pieces of chain.

4) Slide a cloisonné bead and a 5mm Siam bicone on a head pin; form a loop above beads. Trim excess wire. Repeat once.

5) Open a jump ring and slide on end links of one 2¾-inch chain and one 2¼-inch chain; attach jump ring to one outer ring on chandelier component. Repeat for opposite ends of chain on opposite side of chandelier component.

6) Open a loop on one end of the beaded chain from step 2 and connect it to the one outer ring on chandelier component. Repeat for opposite side of beaded chain on opposite side of chandelier component.

7) Open loop on beaded head pin and attach to centre ring on chandelier component.

8) Open ear wire loop and slide on top ring of chandelier component.

9) Repeat steps 5 to 8 for a second earring. ■

Forbidden City
Chandelier components, head pins, gold wire, chain and jump rings from Beadalon; cloisonné beads from Fire Mountain Gems and Beads.

LOOPY TUESDAY

These freeform glass loops have an organic appeal. Adding subtle pearls brings out the beautiful ivory shades, providing a natural complement for brass chain and findings.

Design | Barb Switzer

Skill Level
Intermediate

Finished Size
1¾ inches long

Materials
8 (5mm) champagne freshwater pearls
2 silver and ivory glass links
8 (24-gauge) brass head pins
2 brass ear wires
2 (1½-inch) lengths brass-plated chain
Round-nose pliers
Chain-nose pliers
Flush cutters

Instructions
1) Slide a pearl onto a head pin. Form a wrapped loop, wrapping loop onto top of pearl. Trim excess wire.

2) Slide a pearl onto another head pin and form a wrapped loop in the same manner as before, attaching loop to previous loop before wrapping. Trim excess wire.

3) Repeat step 2 two more times. All four dangles are attached to each other, creating a cluster.

4) Open loop on ear wire and slide on first wrapped loop from step 1. Slide end link of one length of chain onto loop.

5) Thread chain through glass link and attach other end chain link to ear-wire loop. Close loop.

6) Repeat steps 1 to 5 for second earring. ■

Loopy Tuesday
Glass links from Cindy Gimbrone Beads; pearls and head pins from Fusion Beads; chain and ear wires from Fire Mountain Gems and Beads.

WATERFALL CLUSTERS

These earrings use waterfall spacer bars as the foundation for hanging the tiny drop beads. They are a little time consuming to make but worth the effort.

Design | Carole Rodgers

Skill Level
Easy

Finished Size
3 inches long

Materials
72 purple AB drop beads
18 (5-hole) silver waves
   spacer bars
Silver jump rings: 78
   (4mm), 18 (3mm)
2 silver ear wires
2 pairs chain-nose pliers

Note
Use both pairs of chain-nose pliers to open jump rings.

Instructions

1) Open a 4mm jump ring and place a drop bead on it; leave ring open. Repeat for remaining 71 drop beads. Set aside.

2) On one spacer bar, attach a bead jump ring to one end hole and the three middle holes, alternating sides

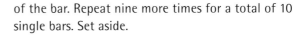

of the bar. Repeat nine more times for a total of 10 single bars. Set aside.

3) On one spacer bar, attach a bead jump ring to each of the three middle holes, alternating sides of the bar. Repeat seven more times for a total of eight bars. Set aside.

4) Use a 3mm jump ring to attach end hole of one single bar to end hole of one bar from step 3.

5) Repeat step 4 three times for a total of four double bars.

6) Use a 3mm jump ring to attach one single bar to end hole of a double bar to create one triple bar.

7) Attach a bead jump ring to each 3mm jump ring used to attach spacer bars together.

8) Use a 3mm jump ring at the end of each bar to attach one single bar, one double bar, one triple bar, one double bar and one single bar to a closed 4mm jump ring.

9) Attach closed 4mm jump ring to another 4mm jump ring; attach second 4mm jump ring to a third 4mm jump ring. Attach last ring to ear wire.

10) Repeat steps 4 to 9 for second earring. ■

Waterfall Clusters
Waves spacer bars, jump rings and ear wires from Beadalon.

MARGUERITE

Marguerite is sophisticated but not stuffy—fun but not fluffy. Sterling silver links support mixed aqua crystals and blush pearls.

Design | Molly Schaller

Skill Level
Easy

Finished Size
3¼ inches long

Materials
2 (4mm) bronze CRYSTALLIZED™ - Swarovski Elements crystal pearls
CRYSTALLIZED™ - Swarovski Elements crystals: 2 (8mm) mint alabaster helix, 2 (6mm) pacific opal round
2 (17 x 10mm) sterling silver swirl links
6 silver ball-tip head pins
2 (4mm) silver jump rings
2 silver ear wires
8 inches sterling silver chain
Round-nose pliers
Chain-nose pliers
Flush cutters

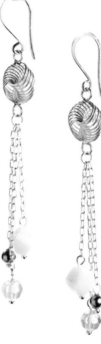

Instructions
1) Cut chain as follows: two 1-inch pieces, two 1¼-inch pieces and two 1½-inch pieces.

2) Slide one helix crystal onto a head pin; form a loop. Trim excess wire. Repeat for each crystal and pearl.

3) Open loops on beaded head pins. Attach helix crystals to 1-inch chains, pearls to 1¼-inch chains and round crystals to 1½-inch chains.

4) Open one jump ring; slide end links of three chains, one of each length, onto jump ring. Attach ring to a spiral link; close ring. Repeat once.

5) Open loops on ear wires and slide on opposite loops of spiral links; close loops. ■

Marguerite
Crystals and crystal pearls from CRYSTALLIZED™ –
Swarovski Elements; swirl links and chain from
Fire Mountain Gems and Beads; head pins and
jump rings from Beadalon.

JET BICONE DANGLES

Sleek formality is encapsulated by black bicone crystals and sterling silver. Stack them long for extra drama or shorter for versatility.

Design | Sandy Parpart

Skill Level
Easy

Finished Size
3 inches long

Materials
10 (8mm) black CRYSTALLIZED™ - Swarovski Elements bicone crystals
2 (2-inch) 24-gauge sterling silver head pins
8 (2-inch) 24-gauge sterling silver eye pins
2 sterling silver fishhook ear wires
Round-nose pliers
Needle-nose pliers
Wire nippers

Instructions

1) Slide a bicone crystal onto a head pin; form a wrapped loop. Trim excess wire.

2) Open loop on an eye pin and attach to previous wrapped loop. String a bicone crystal. Form a wrapped loop; trim excess wire.

3) Repeat step 2 three more times.

4) Open loop on ear wire and attach to previous wrapped loop; close loop.

5) Repeat steps 1 to 4 for second earring. ■

Jet Bicone Dangles
All materials from Fusion Beads.

STARBURSTS

Light, romantic and fun, sterling silver earrings sparkle with crystal accents. AB-finished crystals give a rainbow of fiery contrast to shiny hammered accents.

Design | Camilla Jorgensen

Skill Level
Easy

Finished Size
2 inches long

Materials
42 (4mm) light sapphire AB2X CRYSTALLIZED™ - Swarovski Elements biconc crystals
4 (8 x 14mm) sterling silver 2-hole hammered oval links
42 (½-inch) sterling silver ball-tip head pins
6 (5mm) sterling silver jump rings
2 (8mm) sterling silver hammered earring studs
Round-nose pliers
2 pairs of chain-nose pliers
Flush cutters

Instructions

1) Slide a light sapphire crystal onto a head pin. Form a loop above crystal; trim excess wire. Repeat for each crystal.

2) Use both pairs of chain-nose pliers to open a jump ring. Slide seven beaded head pins and one hammered oval (convex side out) onto ring; close jump ring.

3) Open another jump ring and slide on seven beaded head pins and another hammered oval (convex side out); slide jump ring through top hole of hammered oval from step 2. Close ring.

4) Open another jump ring and slide on seven beaded head pins; slide jump ring through top hole of second hammered oval and loop on ear stud. Close jump ring.

5) Repeat steps 2 to 4 for second earring. ■

Starbursts

CRYSTALLIZED™ - Swarovski Elements
bicone crystals and sterling silver
findings from Frabels Inc.; sterling silver
hammered ovals from Somerset Silver Inc.

EMPEROR'S GARDEN

The cloisonné butterfly beads bring beauty to this Chinese-inspired design.

Design | Candie Cooper

Skill Level
Intermediate

Finished Size
2½ inches long

Materials
2 (18mm) cloisonné
   butterfly beads
CRYSTALLIZED™ - Swarovski Elements bicone crystals:
   4 (3mm) smoked topaz AB, 2 (4mm) topaz
4 (3mm) silver round beads
4 (3mm) silver jump rings
2 (14.8mm) 2-to-1 silver chandelier components
6 (2-inch) silver eye pins
2 (2-inch) silver head pins
2 silver French ear wires
2 inches 2.3mm silver cable chain
Round-nose pliers
Chain-nose pliers
Wire nippers

Notes
If 2-to-1 chandelier components cannot be found, modify 3- or 4-to-1 components by snipping off extra loops. If holes in butterfly beads are too large, insert a small piece of clear rubber tubing inside hole to make hole smaller.

Instructions

1) String one silver round bead, butterfly bead and a silver round bead on a head pin; form a loop above beads. Trim excess wire. Repeat once.

2) String one smoked topaz AB bicone on an eye pin; form a loop after bead, positioning loop so it is perpendicular to eye-pin loop. Trim excess wire. Repeat three additional times.

3) String one topaz bicone on an eye pin; form a loop above bead in the same manner as in step 2. Trim excess wire. Repeat once.

4) Cut eight 2-link sections of silver chain.

5) Open a jump ring and slide on one section of chain; attach ring to one outer loop on chandelier finding. Open loop on a smoky topaz link and attach to end of previous chain; close loop. Open opposite loop on same eye pin and attach to another 2-link section of chain.

6) Repeat step 5 for opposite outer loop on chandelier finding.

7) Open one loop on topaz link and slide on end links of chain; close loop.

8) Open loop on a butterfly dangle and attach to bottom loop of chandelier finding; close loop. Open loop on topaz link and attach to ear wire loop; close loop.

9) Repeat steps 5 to 8 for a second earring. ■

Emperor's Garden
Chandelier components, head pins, chain and jump rings from Beadalon; cloisonné beads from Fire Mountain Gems and Beads.

SIAM STUNNERS

You're sure to get noticed in these swingy stunners! And they're easy to make—just add a few sparkly dangles, some chain and ear wires, and you're done!

Design | Katie Hacker

Skill Level
Intermediate

Finished Size
3½ inches long

Materials
CRYSTALLIZED™ - Swarovski Elements bicone crystals: 8 (4mm) light Siam, 6 (6mm) Siam

2 (8mm) clear AB CRYSTALLIZED™ - Swarovski Elements clear doughnut crystals

4 (8mm) CRYSTALLIZED™ - Swarovski Elements light Siam/silver bead caps

2 CRYSTALLIZED™ - Swarovski Elements silver teardrop earring components with 7 bottom loops and Siam and light Siam crystals

10 silver head pins

2 silver eye pins

8 silver jump rings

2 silver ear wires

7 inches small silver cable chain

Round-nose pliers

Chain-nose pliers

Wire nippers

Instructions
1) Open loops on ear wires and attach to top loops of teardrop earring components; close loops.

2) Slide a Siam bicone crystal and a light Siam crystal on a head pin; form a loop above top bead. Trim excess wire. Repeat three additional times. Open loops and attach to left- and right-side bottom loops on earring components; close loops.

3) Cut four ½-inch lengths of chain.

4) Slide a light Siam bicone crystal on a head pin; form a loop above crystal. Trim excess wire. Open loop and attach to end link of a ½-inch chain; close loop. Repeat to attach a beaded head pin to end link of three remaining ½-inch chains.

5) Use jump rings to attach end links of chains to loops next to side bottom loops of earring components.

6) Slide a bead cap, clear doughnut crystal and a bead cap on an eye pin. *Note: Bead caps should cup the crystal.* Form a loop above top bead cap; trim excess wire. Slide a Siam bicone crystal on a head pin; form a loop above crystal. Trim excess wire. Open loop and attach to bottom loop of beaded eye pin; close loop.

7) Repeat step 6.

8) Open top loops of beaded eye pins and attach to centre bottom loops of earring components; close loops.

9) Cut two 2½-inch chains. Use jump rings to attach end links of chains to remaining bottom loops of earring components. ∎

Siam Stunners
CRYSTALLIZED™ - Swarovski Elements crystals and earring components from Pure Allure; chain and findings from Beadalon.

HYACINTH HONEY

This pair of earrings with delicate floral dangles studded with crystals is easy to create and will always look gorgeous.

Design | Rupa Balachandar

Skill Level
Easy

Finished Size
2 inches long

Materials
2 (10mm) hyacinth CRYSTALLIZED™ - Swarovski Elements 2-loop floral drops
2 (10mm) peach/hyacinth CRYSTALLIZED™ - Swarovski Elements five-petal flowers
2 (5mm) antique-finish jump rings
2 antique gold-finish lever-back ear wires
Flat-nose pliers
Chain-nose pliers

Instructions
1) Open one jump ring and slide it onto one of the loops on back of peach/hyacinth flower and one loop of hyacinth drop; close ring. Repeat once.

2) Open loops on ear wires and slide on top loops of hyacinth drops; close loops. ■

SHELL EARRINGS

White is essential, pure and goes with everything. Beautiful coin shell beads are stunning with a dash of small beads and shining silver.

Design | Helen Rafson

Skill Level
Beginner

Finished Size
2½ inches long

Materials
2 (15mm) white shell coin beads
6 (3mm) silver round beads
20 white seed beads
4 silver spacers
2 silver head pins
2 silver French ear wires
Round-nose pliers
Chain-nose pliers
Wire nippers

Instructions

1) String the following onto a head pin: silver round bead, silver spacer, white shell coin, silver spacer, silver round bead, 10 white seed beads and a silver round bead. Form a loop. Trim excess wire. Repeat once.

2) Open loops on ear wires and slide on beaded head pins. ■

MERMAID'S SCALES

Gold jump rings hold blue lentil beads, in graduated hues, to a chain that creates movement and draws attention to the wearer. Vermeil ear threads finish the look.

Design | Molly Schaller

Skill Level
Easy

Finished Size
3 inches long

Materials
6mm lentil beads: 4 Capri blue, 6 teal matte AB, 6 peridot matte AB

16 (3mm) gold jump rings

2 (3-inch) vermeil ear threads with box and cable chain

2 pairs of chain-nose pliers

Instructions
1) Using both pairs of chain-nose pliers, open all 16 jump rings.

2) Slide one Capri blue lentil bead onto an open jump ring and attach it to top ring of ear thread's chain, closing it with chain-nose pliers.

3) Repeat step 2 with a second Capri blue lentil, attaching it to third link of chain, but on opposite side of chain link.

4) Continue attaching lentils in this manner (three teal matte lentils and then three peridot lentils), to every other link of chain, alternating sides, from top to bottom.

5) Repeat steps 1 to 4 for a second earring. ■

Mermaid's Scales
Lentil beads from Fusion Beads;
jump rings from Beadalon; ear
threads from Rings & Things.

BEACH FUN

Light, romantic and fun, these sterling silver earrings will have you thinking of sunny spring afternoons spent strolling along the beach without a care in the world.

Design | Camilla Jorgensen

Skill Level
Easy

Finished Size
1½ inches long

Materials
2 (13mm) sterling silver starfish charms
2 (5mm) sterling silver jump rings
2 (27mm) sterling silver open rings with 1 hole
2 (8mm) sterling silver hammered square earring studs
2 (6-inch) lengths 2mm oval sterling silver chain
Round-nose pliers
Flat-nose pliers
Flush cutters

Instructions

1) Use both pairs of pliers to open one jump ring. Slide one end of one 6-inch chain onto jump ring; randomly wrap chain around one sterling silver open ring. Thread jump ring through hole at top of open ring; attach end of chain to jump ring.

2) Slide one starfish onto jump ring. Thread jump ring through loop on ear stud. Close ring.

3) Repeat steps 1 and 2 for second earring. ■

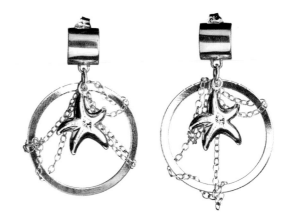

Beach Fun
All materials from Fire
Mountain Gems and Beads.

PEACE PEARLS

It takes many years to grow a fruitful olive tree, but only a few minutes to make these classically simple earrings.

Design | Barb Switzer

Skill Level
Easy

Finished Size
2 inches long

Materials
Light green CRYSTALLIZED™ - Swarovski Elements
    crystal pearls: 4 (3mm), 2 (6mm)
6 (1-inch) sterling silver ball-tip head pins
2 (32.3 x 8.3mm) sterling silver olive branch links
2 sterling silver ear wires
Round-nose pliers
Chain-nose pliers
Wire nippers

Instructions

1) Open loop on ear wire and slide on top loop of olive branch; close loop.

2) Slide a 6mm pearl on a head pin; form a wrapped loop, attaching loop to bottom of olive branch before wrapping. Trim excess wire. Repeat two more times with 3mm pearls, attaching them on each side of 6mm pearl.

3) Repeat steps 1 and 2 for second earring. ■

Peace Pearls
All materials from Fusion Beads.

WHISPERING LEAVES

Using an oak leaf paper punch on 36-gauge copper tooling foil will give you a shimmering whisper of leaves to dangle from your ears.

Design | Brenda Morris Jarrett

Skill Level
Intermediate

Finished Size
2¼ inches long

Materials
2 (6mm) green jasper stone heishi
   cylinder beads
4 (4mm) copper rondelles
Copper wire: 2 (2-inch) lengths
   24-gauge, 2 (3-inch) lengths
   20-gauge
2 x 2-inch 36-gauge copper metal tooling foil
Round-nose pliers
Flat-nose pliers
Needle-nose pliers
Wire nippers
Oak leaf punch
Jeweller's hammer
Rubber mallet
Steel bench block

Instructions

1) Punch two leaves from tooling foil. Flatten each leaf gently with flat-nose pliers. Form a small loop at stem end of each leaf.

2) Form a wrapped loop at one end of a 2-inch length of 24-gauge wire. String a copper rondelle, green jasper heishi and a copper rondelle. Form a wrapped loop, attaching loop to small loop on a foil leaf before wrapping. Trim excess wire.

3) Use fine-tip pen to make a small dot 1 inch from end of a 3-inch 20-gauge wire. Form a small loop at end of wire nearest 1-inch mark; use flat-nose pliers to curl wire into a spiral up to 1-inch mark.

4) Place wire on steel block and flatten spiral with chasing hammer. Bend wire around a plastic pen to shape into an ear wire. Bend wire up at straight end with flat-nose pliers approximately ⅛ inch. Lightly tap ear wire with rubber mallet to harden.

5) Referring to photo, use flat-nose pliers to bend spiral to side.

6) Slide beaded dangle onto ear wire, sliding it up behind spiral. Flatten swirl slightly to catch dangle.

7) Repeat steps 2 to 6 for second earring, making this earring a mirror opposite of first earring. ∎

Whispering Leaves

Copper wire and rondelles from Fire Mountain Gems and Beads; green jasper heishi beads from Thunderbird Supply Co.; copper tooling foil from Hobby Lobby Stores Inc.; oak leaf punch from Martha Stewart Crafts.

LUCKY CAT

Conjure up a little good luck to cross your path wearing these playful duster earrings. Black crystals and charming felines pounce, swing and tickle your ears and neck.

Design | Caito Amorose

Skill Level
Intermediate

Finished Size
5 inches long

Materials
Jet CRYSTALLIZED™ - Swarovski Elements crystals:
  14 (6mm) bicone, 12 (6mm) round, 10 (4mm) bicone, 10 (4mm) round
12 sterling silver cat charms
34 sterling silver head pins
12 sterling silver eye pins
12 (6mm) sterling silver oval jump rings
2 sterling silver French hook ear wires
2 (3-inch) lengths sterling silver long cable chain
Round-nose pliers
Chain-nose pliers
Wire nippers

Instructions
1) Slide a 4mm round crystal on a head pin; form a wrapped head-pin loop above bead, attaching loop to first link on one chain before wrapping. Trim excess wire.

2) In the same manner, attach a 4mm bicone head pin and a 6mm bicone head pin to second chain link.

3) Slide a 6mm bicone crystal on an eye pin and attach to third chain link in the same manner as before; use a jump ring to attach a cat charm to bottom of eye pin. Attach a 4mm bicone head pin to other side of third link.

4) Attach a 4mm round head pin and a 6mm round head pin to fourth link.

5) Add a 4mm round head pin to fifth link.

6) Repeat step 3, substituting a 6mm bicone in place of the 4mm bicone and attach these to the next link.

7) Add two 4mm bicone head pins to next link.

8) Add one 6mm round head pin to next link.

9) Repeat step 3, substituting round crystals in place of bicone crystals.

10) Add a 6mm bicone head pin and a 4mm round head pin to next link.

11) Add a 4mm bicone head pin to next link.

12) Skip a link and add a 6mm round head pin to next link.

13) Open a jump ring and slide on a cat charm; attach jump ring to next link.

14) Slide a 6mm bicone crystal on an eye pin; form a wrapped loop after crystal, attaching loop to end chain link before wrapping. Trim excess wire. Use a jump ring to attach a cat charm to bottom loop of eye pin.

15) Slide a 6mm round crystal on a head pin; form a wrapped head-pin loop above bead. Trim excess wire. Repeat with a 6mm round crystal and an eye pin; use a jump ring to attach a cat charm to bottom of eye pin.

16) Slide a 6mm bicone crystal on an eye pin; form a wrapped loop after crystal; trim excess wire. Open bottom loop of eye pin and slide on beaded head and eye pins from step 15; attach loop to first chain link; close loop. Open top loop of eye pin and attach to ear wire; close loop.

17) Repeat steps 1 to 16 for a second earring. ■

Lucky Cat
All materials from Fire Mountain Gems and Beads.

URBAN JUNGLE

Dressed down with your favourite pair of worn-out jeans, or dressed up with an 80s-inspired gold mesh mini dress, these multifunctional earrings are sure to cause quite a stir!

Design | Camilla Jorgensen

Skill Level
Easy

Finished Size
2 inches long

Materials
12 (6mm) lime CRYSTALLIZED™ - Swarovski Elements bicone crystals
12 (6mm) lime freshwater pearls
24 (½-inch) sterling silver head pins
2 (4mm) sterling silver jump rings
2 (10mm) sterling silver earring studs
2 (18 x 15mm) sterling silver toggle clasps
2 (⅞-inch) lengths 2mm oval sterling silver chain
Round-nose pliers
Flat-nose pliers
Flush cutters

Instructions
1) Slide a lime crystal onto a head pin; form a loop. Trim excess wire. Repeat for each crystal and freshwater pearl for a total of 24 dangles.

2) Open loop on a pearl dangle and attach to end link of one chain length; close loop. In the same manner, attach a crystal dangle to next link, a pearl dangle to next link and so on until there are six pearl dangles and six crystal dangles attached to chain. Repeat once.

3) Cut off excess chain attached to toggle bars. *Note: Leave one chain link attached to each toggle bar.*

4) Use both pairs of pliers to open one jump ring and attach to toggle bar; slide jump ring through loop on top crystal dangle on one chain before closing.

5) Open loop on an earring stud and slide onto round half of toggle clasp; close loop. Insert toggle bar with attached dangles through round half of toggle.

6) Repeat steps 4 and 5 for second earring. ■

Urban Jungle
CRYSTALLIZED™ - Swarovski Elements crystals, jump rings, earring studs and chain from Frabels Inc.; clasps from Nina Designs.

ICY HOT CRYSTALS

Show your versatile personality wearing these three-dimensional chandelier sparklers. Icy facets of light shimmer and shine in a design that is hot hot hot!

Design | Caito Amorose

Skill Level
Intermediate

Finished Size
3½ inches long

Materials
24 (6mm) crystal clear
CRYSTALLIZED™ – Swarovski
Elements dice beads
30 (3mm) crystal AB
CRYSTALLIZED™ – Swarovski
Elements bicone crystals
22 (6mm) quartz crystal flat rondelles
6 (2-inch) sterling silver head pins
2 sterling silver ear wires
10 inches 24-gauge sterling silver wire
Round-nose pliers
Chain-nose pliers
Wire nippers

Instructions
1) Cut two 2-inch pieces and four 1½-inch pieces of wire.

2) Form a wrapped loop at one end of one 1½-inch wire. String the following: bicone, rondelle and a dice bead.

Form another wrapped loop. Trim excess wire. The dice end will be top of beaded link. Repeat once.

3) String the following onto a head pin: bicone, rondelle, dice bead, bicone, two rondelles, bicone, dice bead, bicone, two rondelles and a bicone. Form a wrapped loop, attaching loop to bottom of one beaded link from step 2 before wrapping. Trim excess wire.

4) String the following onto a head pin: bicone, rondelle, dice bead, bicone, dice bead, bicone and a dice bead. Form a wrapped loop. Trim excess wire. Repeat once.

5) Form a wrapped loop at one end of a 2-inch wire, attaching loop to a beaded dangle from step 4 before wrapping. Trim excess wire.

6) String a bicone, rondelle and a dice bead onto wire from step 5. Insert wire through top loops of beaded links from step 2. String a dice bead, rondelle and a bicone. Form a wrapped loop, attaching loop to remaining beaded dangle from step 4 before wrapping. Trim excess wire.

7) Open loop on ear wire and slide on empty wrapped loop on beaded link. Close loop.

8) Repeat steps 2 to 7 for second earring. ■

Icy Hot Crystals

All materials from Fire Mountain Gems and Beads.

DANCING STARS

Close your eyes, make a wish and fasten your dreams to a dazzling star!

Design | Caito Amorose

Skill Level
Intermediate

Finished Size
3¾ inches long

Materials
Crystal AB CRYSTALLIZED™ - Swarovski Elements star pendants: 2 (28mm), 6 (20mm)
Golden shadow CRYSTALLIZED™ - Swarovski Elements bicone crystals: 28 (5mm), 64 (3mm)
Gold-filled jump rings: 6 (6mm), 2 (3mm)
2 gold-filled ear wires
2 (½-inch) lengths small gold chain
22 inches 24-gauge gold-filled wire
Round-nose pliers
Chain-nose pliers
Wire nippers

Instructions
1) Cut two 5-inch pieces and four 3-inch pieces of wire.

2) Open a 3mm jump ring and slide on end link of one chain; insert chain through hole at top of 28mm star pendant; slide opposite end of chain onto jump ring. Close ring. Repeat once.

3) Attach a 6mm jump ring to each 20mm star pendant.

4) Form a wrapped loop at one end of a 3-inch wire. String 16 (3mm) bicone crystals. Form a wrapped loop, attaching loop to a 20mm star before wrapping. Bend wire gently to form a crescent shape. Trim excess wire.

5) Repeat step 4.

6) Form a wrapped loop at one end of 5-inch wire, attaching loop to a 20mm star before wrapping.

7) String three 5mm bicone crystals, one beaded crescent, seven 5mm bicone crystals, another beaded crescent and four 5mm bicone crystals. Form a wrapped loop, attaching loop to 28mm star before wrapping. Bend wire gently to form a crescent shape. Trim excess wire.

8) Open loop of an ear wire and attach dangle. Close loop.

9) Repeat steps 4 to 8 for second earring. ∎

EVERGREEN EARRINGS

You can't go wrong transforming a filigree cone into the perfect holiday evergreen. No falling pine needles, trimming or watering required!

Design | Caito Amorose

Skill Level
Intermediate

Finished Size
1⅜ inches long

Materials
74 (3mm) emerald CRYSTALLIZED™ - Swarovski
    Elements bicone crystals
2 (6mm) gold star beads
2 (12mm) gold filigree bead cones
2 gold ear wires
2 gold head pins
2 (18-inch) lengths .15mm monofilament beading thread
Beading needle
Round-nose pliers
Chain-nose pliers
Wire nippers
Bead glue

Instructions
1) Thread beading needle with one length of beading thread.

2) Beginning from inside one bead cone, insert needle through one filigree opening, holding thread tail inside.

3) String a crystal; insert needle back down through cone through same opening. The crystal should be sitting on top of the filigree opening.

4) Secure thread inside cone by tying a double knot. Add a drop of glue to knot; let dry and trim short thread tail. Do not trim long thread tail.

5) Continue repeating steps 2 and 3 to add individual crystals, weaving thread in and out, until all openings on cone are covered.

6) Secure thread inside cone in the same manner as in step 4.

7) Slide a crystal on a head pin; carefully slide straight end of head pin up through bottom of cone.

8) String a star bead. Form a wrapped loop; trim excess wire.

9) Open loop on ear wire; attach loop to wrapped loop on head pin. Close loop.

10) Repeat steps 1 to 9 for second earring. ∎

Evergreen Earrings
All materials from Fire Mountain Gems and Beads.

MODERN HOLLY

Tiny crystal squares and rivoli pendants combined with a vermeil four-petal clover make a deconstructed wreath with a modern twist.

Design | Molly Schaller

Skill Level
Intermediate

Finished Size
2 inches long

Materials
CRYSTALLIZED™ - Swarovski Elements crystal
   pendants: 2 (14mm) crystal Sahara square,
   4 (6mm) Siam circle rivoli
2 (7.5 x 7.5mm) gold vermeil four-petal jump rings
10 (3.5mm) gold jump rings
2 gold-plated ear wires with round bead
4 inches 2.25mm gold-filled flat figure-8 chain
Chain-nose pliers
Wire nippers

Note
Use 3.5mm jump rings throughout unless
otherwise directed.

Instructions

1) Cut chain into the following pieces: two 1-link pieces, two 2-link pieces and two 7-link pieces.

2) Open a jump ring. Slide one end of one 7-link chain onto jump ring; thread chain through a crystal Sahara square pendant. Place opposite end of chain onto jump ring. Attach jump ring to a four-petal jump ring; close ring.

3) Open another jump ring; slide one chain link and one Siam circle rivoli pendant onto jump ring. Close ring. Open another jump ring and slide onto chain link attached to circle pendant; attach jump ring to one side of four-petal jump ring. Close jump ring.

4) Open another jump ring. Slide one end of one 2-link chain and a Siam circle rivoli pendant onto jump ring before closing. Use another jump ring to attach opposite end of chain to other side of four-petal jump ring.

5) Open loop on ear wire and slide onto top of four-petal jump ring; close loop.

6) Repeat steps 2 to 5 for second earring. ■

Modern Holly

CRYSTALLIZED™ - Swarovski Elements pendants
and gold vermeil four-petal jump rings from Fusion
Beads; chain and ear wires from Fire Mountain
Gems and Beads; jump rings from Beadalon.

CUPID WHISPERS

Cupid swings beneath each earlobe murmuring his Valentine's Day endearments.

Design | Caito Amorose

Skill Level
Easy

Finished Size
2 inches long

Materials
2 (4mm) garnet round beads
2 (5.5mm) gold-plated clear rhinestone beads
2 gold-finish pewter Cupid charms
2 gold-filled eye pins
2 gold-filled ear wires
Round-nose pliers
Chain-nose pliers
Wire nippers

Instructions

1) String a garnet bead and a rhinestone bead onto an eye pin. Form a wrapped loop; trim excess wire.

2) Open bottom loop of eye pin and add Cupid charm; close loop.

3) Open loop on one ear wire; slide on top loop of beaded dangle. Close loop.

4) Repeat steps 1 to 3 for second earring. ■

Cupid Whispers
All materials from Fire
Mountain Gems and Beads.

LONG & LACY

Link bead caps together to form shoulder-duster earrings with some swing!

Design | Laurie D'Ambrosio

Skill Level
Easy

Finished Size
3½ inches long

Materials
Round beads: 2 (10mm), 2 (8mm)
6 (15mm) flat bead caps
4 (4mm) jump rings
2 head pins
2 eye pins
2 fishhook ear wires
Round-nose pliers
Chain-nose pliers
Wire nippers

Note
Materials listed above are given for one pair of earrings.

Instructions
1) Open two jump rings and attach to opposite-side holes on a bead cap; slide another bead cap on each jump ring before closing rings securely. Repeat once.

2) Slide a 10mm bead on an eye pin. Form a loop after bead; trim excess wire. Repeat once.

3) Open one loop on each beaded eye pin and attach to ear wires; close loops. Open opposite loops on eye pins and attach each to a top loop on a bead cap; close loops.

4) Slide an 8mm bead on a head pin; form a loop after bead. Trim excess wire. Repeat once. Open loops and attach to bottom bead caps. ■

Long & Lacy
Ear wires, head pins and eye pins from
Cousin Corp. of America; bead caps
from Hirschberg Schutz & Co. Inc.

INDEX

Working 9 to 5

Cindi, 16

Kaia's Dream, 18

Green With Envy, 20

Fabric Love, 22

Hidden Sun, 24

Garden Lantern Hoops, 26

Red Doughnuts, 28

All Wrapped Up, 30

Lhasa Drops, 32

In the Loop, 34

Luxe Lotus, 36

Hoopla, 38

INDEX

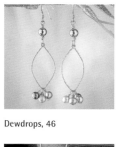

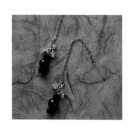

INDEX

INDEX

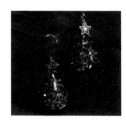

METRIC CONVERSION CHARTS

METRIC CONVERSIONS		
yards x .9144 =	metres (m)	
yards x 91.44 =	centimetres (cm)	
inches x 2.54 =	centimetres (cm)	
inches x 25.40 =	millimetres (mm)	
inches x .0254 =	metres (m)	

centimetres x .3937 =	inches	
metres x 1.0936 =	yards	

INCHES INTO MILLIMETRES & CENTIMETRES (Rounded off slightly)

inches	mm	cm	inches	cm	inches	cm	inches	cm
1/8	3	0.3	5	12.5	21	53.5	38	96.5
1/4	6	0.6	5 1/2	14	22	56	39	99
3/8	10	1	6	15	23	58.5	40	101.5
1/2	13	1.3	7	18	24	61	41	104
5/8	15	1.5	8	20.5	25	63.5	42	106.5
3/4	20	2	9	23	26	66	43	109
7/8	22	2.2	10	25.5	27	68.5	44	112
1	25	2.5	11	28	28	71	45	114.5
1 1/4	32	3.2	12	30.5	29	73.5	46	117
1 1/2	38	3.8	13	33	30	76	47	119.5
1 3/4	45	4.5	14	35.5	31	79	48	122
2	50	5	15	38	32	81.5	49	124.5
2 1/2	65	6.5	16	40.5	33	84	50	127
3	75	7.5	17	43	34	86.5		
3 1/2	90	9	18	46	35	89		
4	100	10	19	48.5	36	91.5		
4 1/2	115	11.5	20	51	37	94		

FEELING CRAFTY? GET CREATIVE!

Each 160-page book features easy-to-follow, step-by-step instructions and full-page colour photographs of every project. Whatever your crafting fancy, there's a Company's Coming Creative Series craft book to match!

Beading: Beautiful Accessories in Under an Hour
Complement your wardrobe, give your home extra flair or add an extra-special personal touch to gifts with these quick and easy beading projects. Create any one of these special crafts in an hour or less.

Knitting: Easy Fun for Everyone
Take a couple of needles and some yarn and see what beautiful things you can make! Learn how to make fashionable sweaters, comfy knitted blankets, scarves, bags and other knitted crafts with these easy-to-intermediate knitting patterns.

Card Making: Handmade Greetings for All Occasions
Making your own cards is a fun, creative and inexpensive way of letting someone know you care. Stamp, emboss, quill or layer designs in a creative and unique card with your own personal message for friends or family.

Patchwork Quilting
In this book full of throws, baby quilts, table toppers, wall hangings—and more—you'll find plenty of beautiful projects to try. With the modern fabrics available, and the many practical and decorative applications, patchwork quilting is not just for Grandma!

Crocheting: Easy Blankets, Throws & Wraps
Find projects perfect for decorating your home, for looking great while staying warm or for giving that one-of-a-kind gift. A range of simple but stunning designs make crocheting quick, easy and entertaining.

Sewing: Fun Weekend Projects
Find a wide assortment of easy and attractive projects to help you create practical storage solutions, decorations for any room or just the right gift for that someone special. Create table runners, placemats, baby quilts, pillows and more!

For a complete listing of Company's Coming cookbooks and craft books, check out

www.companyscoming.com

We have a tasty lineup of cookbooks, with plenty more in the oven.

www.companyscoming.com

- Preview new titles
- Exclusive cookbook offers
- Find titles no longer in stores

Sign up for our FREE newsletter and receive kitchen-tested recipes twice a month!

Company's Coming